Copyright © 2017 by GM Publishers

The copyright of this book is registered by GM Publishers. None can publish this book or part of it without the permission of the publisher or author. No part of this publication may be reproduced, stored in a retrieval system, or transmitted in any form or by any means, electronic, mechanical, photocopying, reading, or otherwise, without the permission of the publishers or author. If anyone copy, publish, print and plagiarized the book will be illegal offence in the eye of law and be punished.

All rights are reserved. Published by GM Publishers

Marketing Strategy & Research
In the Context of Different Organizations

Author: Ghazi Mokammel Hossain

Co-Author: Md. Fazle Mubin

Designer: Ghazi Mokammel Hossain

Publications Format: Kindle E-Book format, Paperback format

Edition No: First Edition, September, 2017

Publication From: UK

Version: International Version

Published by: GM Publishers

ISBN-13: 978-1976123054
ISBN-10: 1976123054

Email address: gmpublishers04@gmail.com

Table of Contents

1.0 Introduction to Strategic Marketing..4
1.1 Types of Markets...5
1.2 Market Segmentation..6
1.3 Marketing Strategy...7
1.4 Marketing Strategy Development Process...8
1.5 Marketing Mix (7Ps)..8
1.6 Marketing Matrix..9
1.6.1 The Ansoff Matrix...10
1.6.2 Boston Growth- Share Matrix...10
1.7 SMART...11
2.0 Analyzing the Marketing Strategy of Different Organizations..............13
2.1 Analyzing the Marketing Strategy of Microsoft & Cargill....................14
2.1.1 Microsoft..14
2.1.2 Cargill..15
2.2 Limitations and Constraints of Marketing..17
2.3.1 SWOT Analysis..21
2.3.2 SMART Objectives..23
2.4 Analyzing the Marketing Environment of Tesco & Oxfam..................25
2.4.1 Tesco..25
2.4.2 Oxfam..27
2.5 Limitations and Constraints of Marketing..28
2.5.1 Limitations and Constraints...28
Sales of Goods Act 1979...28
Consumer Protection from Unfair Trading Regulation 2008.....................29

Consumerism..29
Consumer Protection (Distance selling) Regulation 2000......................30
2.6 Voluntary Code of Advertising in Practice......................................30
2.7 Marketing Research for Marketing Planning..................................31
2.7.1 Impact of Marketing Research in Market Plan............................31
Quantitative and Qualitative Market Research....................................31
Primary & Secondary Market Research..31
2.7.2 Limitations of Marketing Research..32
2.8 Marketing Research Influencing Factors in Marketing....................34
2.9 Implementation, Evaluation & Control in Marketing Plan...............35
2.10 SWOT Analysis..36
Strength..36
Weaknesses..36
Opportunities...37
Threats...37
3.0 Customer Segmentation..37
3.0.1 Benefits of Segmentation..39
3.1 Marketing Mix for a Product...39
3.1.1 Product..40
3.1.2 Price..40
3.1.3 Place...41
3.1.4 Promotion..41
3.2 Coherent Marketing Mix for a Product..41
4.0 References...45
About the Author...48
Also By Ghazi Mokammel Hossain & GM Publishers.........................48

1.0 Introduction to Strategic Marketing

The major approaches that are considered to be the core of the marketing theory and methods are the marketing mix strategy and relationship management. These are often associated with transaction methods and parameter approaches. However, many researchers have view that the marketing theory is now shifting from the mixed approach to the relationship approach of marketing. The encouragement of interaction between the delivered and the customer is seen as the inherent characteristic towards which marketing is shifting.

Many of the traditional strong points of marketing are challenged by the relationship approach to marketing that include the identification of the marketing variables and the existence of the marketing department as an integral part of the organisational solution. On the other hand, some researchers have the view that there is a lack of convincing and well-developed theories of relationship marketing. And this is the actual situation more or less with regards to marketing methods (Czinkota and Kotabe, 2001).

The traditional theories of marketing have undergone some partial changes that have been labelled as relationship marketing argues that despite all modern forms of marketing theories, the constituents of the marketing mix still exist. Any company would require designing, price, distribute, communicate and sell their products. Companies still require staff to be chosen and trained and rewarded for good work and physical surroundings need to be taken into consideration while formulating a marketing strategy. The entire process of marketing management should be planned and implemented accordingly.

1.1 Types of Markets

In the context of marketing, the types of markets are existing market, re-segmented market and new market. But in the context of microeconomics, we can segmented the market in different types as per their characteristics. To solve the confusion, we have discussed the type of markets in the contexts of marketing and microeconomics as well. These are given below:

Types of Markets in the Context of Marketing

Three Types of Markets

	Existing Market	Resegmented Market	New Market
Customers	Existing	Existing	New & New Usage
Customer Needs	Performance	1. Cost 2. Perceived Need	Simplicity & Convenience
Performance	Better/Faster	1. Good enough at the low end 2. Good enough for new niche	Low in "traditional attributes", improved by "new" metrics
Competition	Existing Incumbents	Existing Incumbents	Non-consumption & other startups
Risks	Existing Incumbents	1. Existing Incumbents 2. Niche strategy fails	Market Adoption

Types of Markets in the Context of Microeconomics

4 types of Market Structures	Perfect Competition	Monopolistic Competition	Oligopoly	Monopoly
Number of firms	Many	Several	Few	One
Freedom of entry	Open Access	Open Acess	Controlled Access	Barriers of entry: Technical, legal & economic
Nature of Product	Uniform	Differentiated	Uniform or Differentiated	Specialized
Implications for demand curve	Horizontal line Perfect elastic	Downward sloping (elastic)	Downward sloping (inelastic) Game Theory	Downward sloping - Control over price and is more inelastic compared to Oligopoly - Straight line demand curve (MR 2x steep)
Average size of firms	Small Firms - Small enough that no firm affects the market price or quantities	Small Firms - Extremely competitive small degree of market control	Large in size - dominated	Large in size - provides all of the market's supply
Possible consumer demand	Price is unrelated to the quanity produced/sold	Firms have the ability to control the price somewhat- Competitive goods are close substitutes	Non-price competition - consumers determine how much to buy = firm successful	Demand will not remain constant as the firms increase their output
Profit making possibility	MR=MC Marginal profit is zero TR - TC	MR=MC Makes no economic profit	MR=MC (Cartel & Collusion)	MR=MC Maximizes profits - the price the firm will charge a product at the maximum possible price
Government Intervention	Government Intervention	Government Intervention - Entry can be blocked by the government or regulation	Government Intervention - Collusions are illegal in most countries w/ penalties	Government Intervention - By taxation, price setting & nationalization
Criticism	Ideal - not seen in reality	Advertising	Agreements made between few firms that divide the market up. Agree on quota or a fixed price	Being able to make economic profits in short run and long run -using power to increase price -Inefficient in productivity & allocatively -Higher price for a product & producing a lower output

1.2 Market Segmentation

Market segmentation determines to segment the market by synchronizing the different variables like geographic, demographic, psychographic and behavioral etc. of the market. The discussion of marketing segmentation variables are as follows:

Market Segmentation			
Geographic	**Demographics**	**Psychographic**	**Behavioural**
Grouping customers based on defined geographical boundaries	Grouping customers based on customer personal attributes	Grouping customers according to lifestyles	Grouping customers based on actual customer behaviour toward products and services
For example: • Region • Country • Population • Climate	For example: • Age • Gender • Nationality • Ethnicity • Occupation • Income • Social class • Family size • Religion • Education	For example: • Lifestyle • Personality • Values • Attitudes • Opinions • Interests	For example: • Brand loyalty • Benefits sought • User status • Usage rates • Occasion • Readiness to buy

1.3 Marketing Strategy

Marketing strategy is a set of plan that can help the organization to optimize its product/service performance in the market. It also analyzes the performance of the different departments of an organization who're directly or indirectly involved in the marketing process. Different types of marketing strategies are as follows:

Figure 1: Different Type of Marketing Strategies

1.4 Marketing Strategy Development Process

Marketing strategy development process begins from strategic analysis and ends at the strategy implementation some other factors are also included in the middle of these process. Marketing Strategy Development process are as follow:

Figure 2: **Marketing Strategy Development from Stage 1 to 6**

1.5 Marketing Mix (7Ps)

Different elements are directly or indirectly related to the marketing process of a product/service of the company in the market. All these factors or elements influence the consumer to purchase the product or service, these influencing factors/elements are called marketing mix. The elements of marketing mix are as follows:

Figure 3: Marketing Mix (7Ps)

1.6 Marketing Matrix

Some matrix are directly related to the marketing concepts and theories. Within all of these, The Ansoff Matrix and BCG-Share Matrix have been achieved more popularity because of their effectiveness in the marketing performance analysis and strategy formulation. These are discussed in the following segment:

1.6.1 The Ansoff Matrix

Ansoff matrix plays an enormous role in the formulation of effective marketing strategy for any types of organization.

In 1957, Russian American Igor Ansoff was developed this concept for effective product marketing. It has been analyzed below:

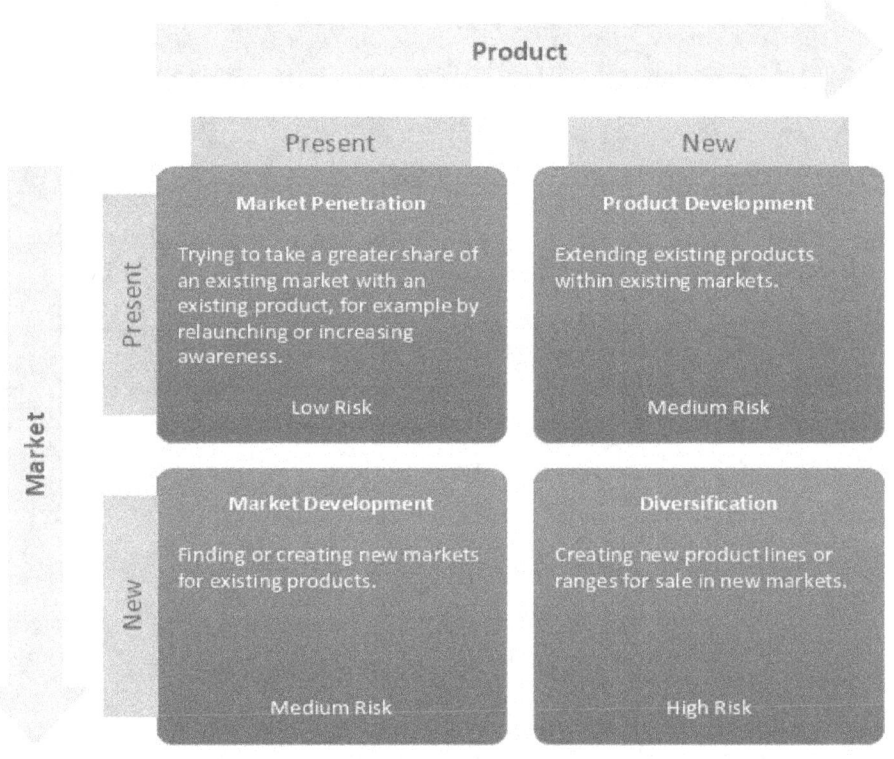

Figure 4: The Ansoff Matrix

1.6.2 Boston Growth- Share Matrix

Another popular matrix that's generally implemented for the marketing strategy formulation is called BCG-Matrix.

In 1970, this matrix was developed by Bruce D. Henderson for Boston Consulting Growth to analyze the product management, strategic management, brand marketing, and portfolio of different corporations. At present, most of the corporate organizations are using BCG-Matrix to formulate and analyze the performance of the management and marketing departments. BCG-Matrix is determined below:

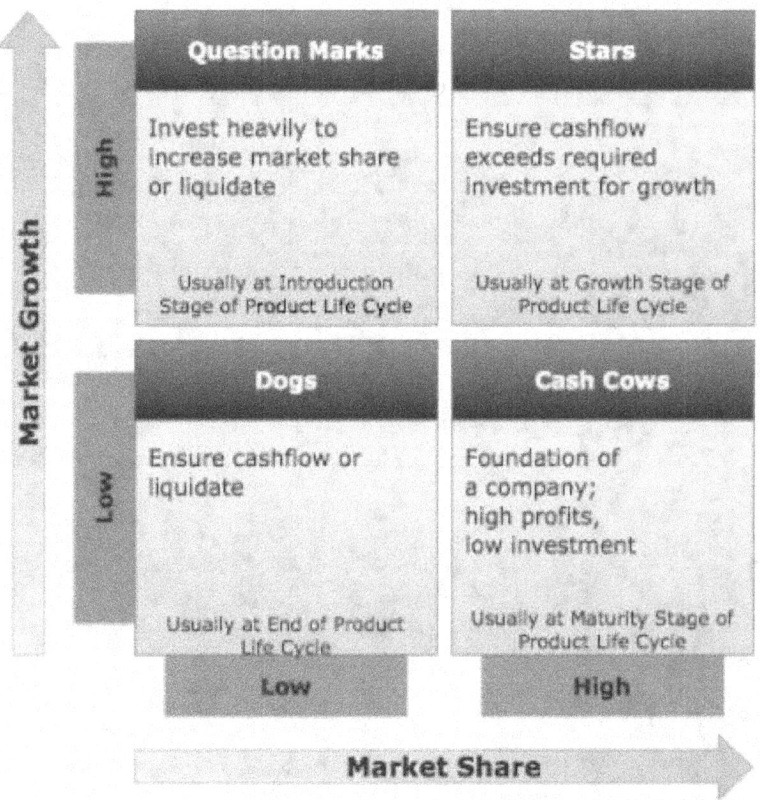

Figure 5: BCG-Matrix

1.7 SMART

At present, SMART is the popular approach of strategic marketing.

The abbreviation of SMART is Specific, Measurable, Attainable, Relevant, Timely. Most of the corporate organizations are now rely on SMART to formulate their marketing goals and strategies. Detail discussion is as follows:

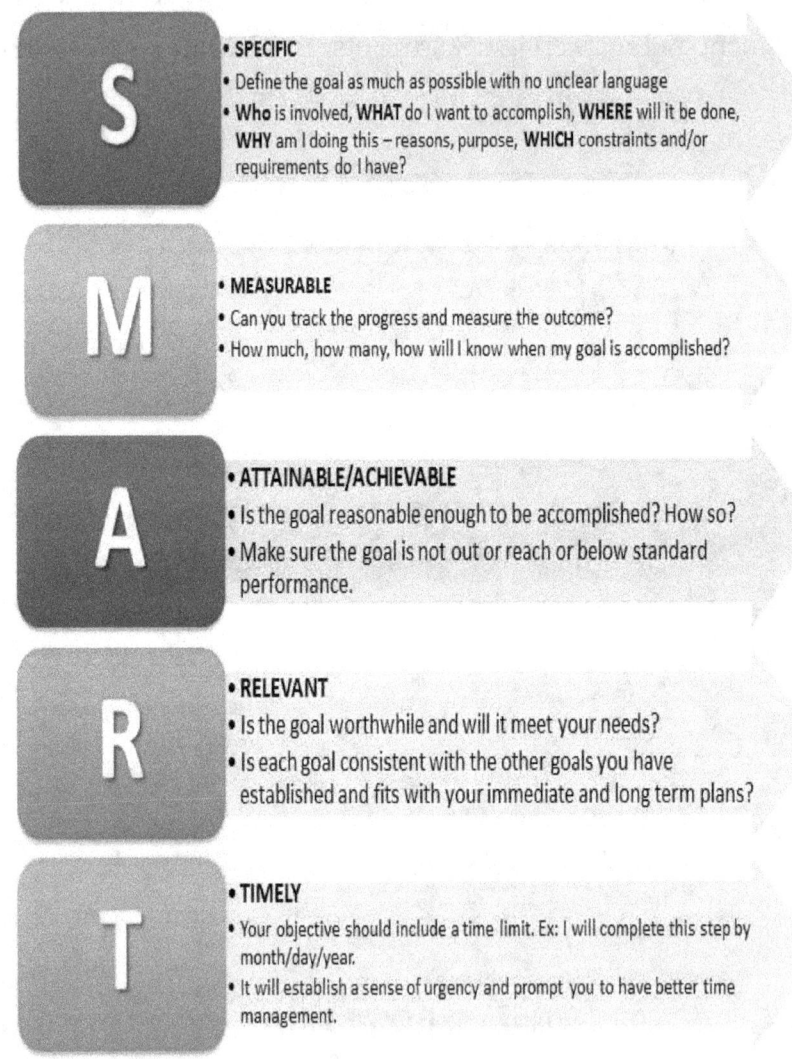

2.0 Analyzing the Marketing Strategy of Different Organizations

In the section one, we discussed about the theoretical aspect of marketing and its different strategies. Now we are going to analyze the real life strategic marketing of four different organizations such as, Microsoft, Cargill, Tesco and Oxfam. In this analysis, we've compared the strategic marketing process of Microsoft and Cargill.

In the same way, we've differentiated the marketing process of Tesco and Oxfam. Before the beginning, we want to clarify you that we have only been added Microsoft and Tesco's marketing research sections. But we haven't been added the marketing research sections for the Oxfam and Cargill as the both organizations aren't done marketing research activities so effectively like the other two organizations. We should keep in mind that Oxfam is a non-profitable organization, thus they are done less marketing research activities. In contrary, Cargill is related with various industries such as, trading, agriculture, energy, livestock, food, finance etc. For that reason, it's hard for us to identify their marketing research job for the particular industries.

The goal of this section is to identify the connection between practical and theoretical aspects of strategic marketing. This will help us to know whether or not our theoretical learning on strategic marketing are implemented in the real life corporate giants or the non-profitable organization marketing strategy formulation.

2.1 Analyzing the Marketing Strategy of Microsoft & Cargill

Marketing is a necessary part of business in the present business environment. Without marketing activities, none of the business organization can reach its goals (Dann and Dann, 2004). Marketing is also called a profit generation strategy for the business organizations. The marketing techniques used by Microsoft (Public sector) and Cargill (Private sector) are given below:

2.1.1 Microsoft

a. **Growth strategies:** Microsoft intends to boost its business growth by developing its products like Windows or office and also by improving its rate of acquisition.
b. **Survival strategies:** Learning from many of the flaws of its products Microsoft is trying to diminish their limitations. And by adding more services it intends to create a big impact in the marketing world (Lewis, 1999).
c. **Branding:** By creating a Business to Business (B2B) relationship with other companies and by being a trustworthy company themselves they have excelled in branding (Lewis, 1999). And also through innovative ads they are now one of the top companies in the world.

d. **Relationship marketing:** By being a trustworthy and profitable source other companies and enterprises is trying to Add Microsoft as a permanent business partner. And this aspect helps in their relationship marketing plan (Microsoft.com, 2017).

2.1.2 Cargill

a. **Growth strategies:** Since the diversity of products of Cargill are so vast, it can grow in many sectors by improving and modifying their products especially the most demanded ones (Cargill.com, 2017).

b. **Survival strategies:** To survive in the marketing world, Cargill is creating a vast network with various buyers to supply their products. The bigger the network, the better is their chance of survival (Cargill.com, 2017).

c. **Branding:** As they have a variety of products they do not have any problems with branding their company's name (Dann and Dann, 2004). By making a vast impact on the marketing world they are already renowned. And they are further improved by trading and selling their products all over the world.

d. **Relationship marketing:** Cargill makes a variety of products they have a huge number of buyers and consumers and so by making profits and trading their products in more than 10 countries like China, Japan, Australia, they are planning to improve their marketing relationship (Cargill.com, 2017).

Now a comparison of the marketing techniques of the two organizations (Microsoft and Cargill) is given below:

Topic	Microsoft	Cargill
1. Growth Strategies	By developing its most demanded products and improving its rate of acquisition.	By improving and modifying its diverse supplies, especially the most demanded ones
2. Survival Strategies	They want to add more profitable services and diminishing the limitations and flaws of their products.	They want to create a vast business network around the world to supply their products.
3. Branding	They are creating a business to business relationship with other companies and trying be a trustworthy source of profit	Improving their trade business and sales all over the world they are trying to brand their names

4.Relationship Marketing	They are trying to be a trustworthy and profitable source so that other companies and enterprises want to add Microsoft as a permanent business partner.	They have a huge number of buyers and consumers and so by making profits and trading their products in more than 10 countries, they will try to make the best of this opportunity to improve their marketing relationship

The effectiveness of different product marketing strategies of Microsoft is given below:

Although the marketing strategies of Microsoft is not perfect than Cargill but still it is very effective. By using them, Microsoft has become one of the best companies in the world. They are earning a lot of profit from some of their major products like OS (Windows) and Microsoft Office and from other services like Skype, OneDrive which they have recently bought (Microsoft.com, 2017).

2.2 Limitations and Constraints of Marketing

The limitations and constraints of marketing for Microsoft is given below:
- ➢ **Legal constraints**: The legal constraints that Microsoft faced was;
- **Sales of goods act 1979:** According to this act the goods sold to the customer should be as promised and in good working quality.

Up to this time, there are no major record of Microsoft colliding with this act (Microsoft.com, 2017).

- **Consumer protection from unfair trading regulation 2008:** The main goal of this law is for the traders to act fairly towards the customers. And so far Microsoft had no problem involving this law.

➢ **Voluntary constraints:** The voluntary constraints that may be faced is that according to the voluntary code of their advertisement must be decent and not offensive in anyway, it cannot contain anything that makes the consumers break the law in anyway (Microsoft.com, 2017).

➢ **Pressure groups and consumerism:** According to consumerism act, Microsoft must produce products of good quality and must consider that the products should be safe (Microsoft.com, 2017). And if there are any complaints by the customers it is the duty of Microsoft to listen to them and act accordingly.

➢ **Acceptable language:** Since Microsoft is an internationally renowned company it is trying and yet to make their products in different major languages like Arabic, Bengali, Hindi, Mandarin, etc.

2.3 Marketing Research of Microsoft

Microsoft uses marketing research to contribute to the development of its marketing plans in the following ways:

Quantitative and qualitative market research: By researching different research surveys Microsoft has found that they can develop their marketing plans by extending their platform through Office, Xbox, Skype and many other offerings of Microsoft. Moreover, by developing their sales of demanding products like office, Windows, etc. (Microsoft.com, 2017). It can help them to reach their goals as well.

Primary and secondary market research: The primary market research conducted by Microsoft is to monitor and report on the competitive activity and performance and the trending of their major products (Microsoft.com, 2017). The secondary market research conducted by them is to identify resources to gain relevant data to support the growth of new market opportunities.

Uses and limitations of market research

By researching they can focus on their products, technologies and advertisements and obtain technical insights to drive business decision making. And the limitations of their marketing research are they not provide new services in any of their products such as Office. If we notice we can understand that the new updates of the office only contains graphical improvement but do not have any additional services.

This might be a result of lack of proper market research. How Microsoft uses the limitations of marketing research to contribute to the development of a selected organization's marketing plan is given below:

Cost effectiveness: Microsoft has been working on many plans to improve the cost effectiveness of their products and services which they have like Hybrid cloud, Windows server 2012 R2, Office 365, Microsoft Azure and many more. These products are providing quality services at low costs (Microsoft.com, 2017).

Validity data collected: From various surveys and researches Microsoft has found out that some of the data collected by them were out of date including products like Windows, Office. And by refining their data's, they intend to improve their marketing plans. How Microsoft uses marketing research for its marketing planning is given below:

Marketing Planning Process Model: The marketing planning process model of Microsoft includes-

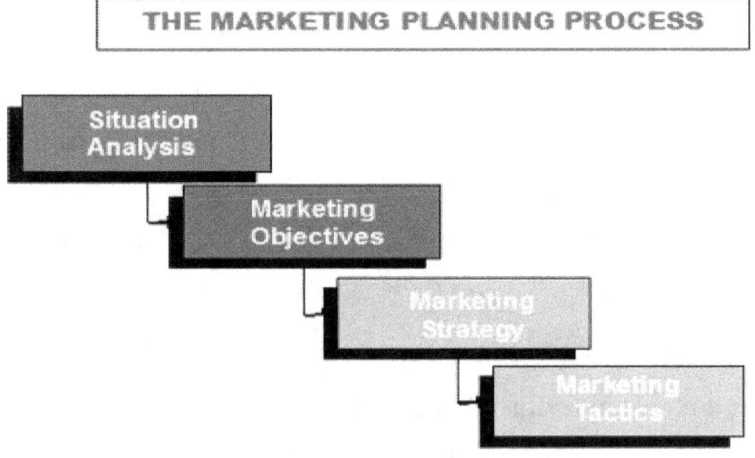

Figure 6: The Marketing Process Model

a) **Situation analysis:** By analyzing the situation and state of the market they supply their goods so that when the demand is more the supplies are in the right amount too.

b) **Marketing objectives:** In the beginning of every year Microsoft makes some mandatory marketing objectives like a setting up definite sale rate and a definite profit rate. They work accordingly to complete these objectives and some optional objectives too (Microsoft.com, 2017).

c) **Marketing strategies:** To make a good marketing strategy they have created a bond with difference financial, educational, and cultural and also many voluntary organizations. Moreover, they have ERGs (Employee Resource groups) and ENs (Employee Networks)

d) **Marketing tactics:** Microsoft has many of the best marketing tacticians in the world and so they are pulling off many unexpected wonders, for example the case with the "Destiny the game". Except that some strategies by Microsoft are technology accessibility option, promoting many advertisements via important organization, building a healthy and collaborative relationship with other companies etc. (Microsoft.com, 2017).

2.3.1 SWOT Analysis

Strength:
- It is one of the Leading Companies in the world

- It has worldwide marketing connection in almost all the countries of the world and many major companies
- Their technologies like Office, Windows (OS) etc. are used by many institutions and organization (Microsoft.com, 2017).

Weakness:
- One of the unsuccessful project of Microsoft is their Bing search engine and they're losing a lot of money for this project in every year.
- The browser of Microsoft is a major downfall because of the rise of some of the more popular browsers like Mozilla, Chrome etc.
- The Windows Phone market was overtaken by Apple's iPhone and Android smartphone, thus it is not so famous worldwide.

Opportunities:
- Increasing the production of the major products like Office, Windows (OS).
- Branding and advertising through major companies like NVidia, AMD etc.
- Buying shares and programs like Skype (Microsoft.com, 2017).

Threats:
- Incurring loss from many unpopular products.

- Not adding additional services with major products.
- Not including major languages like Bengali, Urdu, Persian and many other languages in their products.

2.3.2 SMART Objectives

a. **Specific:** In Microsoft's area of focus, they want to include the major languages in the world in their main products and software.

b. **Meaningful:** This goal is important for Microsoft because if they don't, they will have a major fall out in their sales and trading (Microsoft.com, 2017).

c. **Action oriented:** The steps that are taken by Microsoft is including the Mandarin in their top products and services and are looking forward to adding more languages.

d. **Realistic**: They want to achieve this goal in such a way that their products can be used by all the people in the world despite their difference of use of language (Microsoft.com, 2017).

e. **Time:** They want to achieve this goal between the years 2020-25.

Six different customer groups that are targeted by Microsoft for selected their products are:

- ➢ **Software Companies (B2B):** Microsoft has made a partnership with companies like NVidia, AMD, etc. By including their products like Windows (OS) to other company's products they are able to advertise and branding (Microsoft.com, 2017).

- **Financial Organizations (B2B):** The Windows (OS) are used by many banks, which make them a potential target. These help in the increase of demand of their products.
- **Technological Companies (B2B):** Companies like Intel, HP, and Samsung are the beneficial partner and can help a lot to attain their financial and sales goals (Järvinen and Taiminen, 2015).
- **Educational Institutions (B2C):** The educational institutions like Harvard, MIT, Princeton, Oxford, etc. can help them by promoting their products to the students as well as the teachers. And so they are the major sources (Wood, 2012).
- **Voluntary Organizations (B2C):** Organizations which are based on voluntary works like helping refugees e.g. IOM, helping the war affected people e.g. UNHCR etc. are an important target of Microsoft (Järvinen and Taiminen, 2015).
- **General Consumers (B2C):** The general people are very important because they are the reason for the popularity of some of their major products and services like Office, Windows, and Skype etc. Gamers, Programmers, Businessman fall in this category (Wood, 2012).

Justified recommendations for improving the validity of the marketing research used to contribute to the development of Microsoft's marketing plans are given below:

The Amount of people to question: Invalid data collected my marketing research can cause major loss so Microsoft must question the right amount of people to avoid this damage and the information and the data collected must be valid and up to date (Lewis, 1999).

Correct information: They should gather correct information from various sources like students, programmers, businessmen and other groups of consumers (Lewis, 1999). By doing this they will be able to gather infarctions on the products which they should concentrate on more and also increase the production of.

Learning from Complaints: Microsoft's products have many limitations and issues. By gathering complaints from various groups of consumers they can learn what to improve on their products and also what problems they have to overcome.

One of the examples is the Office, though on updated versions of it, they have improved the graphics they have not included many required systems (Microsoft.com, 2017). This is a major drawback and so from these complaints they can build an even stronger marketing plan.

2.4 Analyzing the Marketing Environment of Tesco & Oxfam

2.4.1 Tesco

Tesco is one of the largest and most resourceful supermarket chains in the UK.

Tesco has efficiently penetrated the global market and operating a successful business operation all over the world. The organisation has extended its business operation into 12 countries including Czech Republic, Ireland, Hungary, Poland, Malaysia, China and India. The mission and objective of Tesco are to develop excellent shopping experience and maximum customer loyalty.

The organisation is always aggressive in establishing a higher standard of a goal to grow sustainably in this globalised platform. The organisation is continuously adapting to the situational and environment changes in the market for a profitable and successful business operation (Boothby, 2007). The process of globalisation has created a diverse competitive platform for the organisations, for which the organisation has to change or alter their strategic policies to sustain successfully.

Tesco with its adaptive nature has made various changes and implemented several innovative planning in the various segment of their business operation. Therefore, the perspective of the market plan changes according to the prospect of the market. The requirement of the customer is changing day by day, as because of the changing environment and trend of the market (Rossiter, 2002).

The most important element of marketing strategies of Tesco is to sustain and carry forward their brand image for long term goal. The nature of the trade of Tesco has made the process of marketing easier. The company is everywhere, sell everything to everyone has made the business reach every corner of the globe.

In the process of marketing a product or service, the corporation implemented certain policies depending on the evaluation of the internal and external aspect to have an advantageous business in this competitive market. The organisation has designed their planning in such a manner so that it completely matches with the requirements of the customers. Tesco as compared to the other companies has given higher precedence to the quality of their product and services. In marketing management, Tesco has created a structure with different intensity of customers according to their monetary status.

2.4.2 Oxfam

Oxfam is a voluntary sector, relies mainly on the donation and volunteers for their organisational operation. The main function and objective of this establishment are to provide a solution to the issues faced by the different communities in the world which include poverty, issues related to health, injustice and calamities. The target market gives emphasis on people who need help and primarily dependent on the NGOs. The organisation deals with mainly education, health and family unit.

The improvement of the organisation is inclined by the different political issues happening all over the globe like violence and wars. The organisation promotes their advocacies which are emphasised by diverse marketing solutions. The organisation for sustainable development aligned with 14 other groups which have same purpose and activity. The organisation works for individuals of every age, different community and background. To enhance the quality of living standard in a safe environment, the organisation gives emphasis on publicity, integrating advertising, promotions and creating awareness among the communities (Campaignlive.co.uk, 2015).

The main prospect of Oxfam includes increasing the level of donation, volunteers and international partnership to reach every unreached area of the world suffering from various issues. The marketing method and approach for the sustainable development are creating awareness through educating and awareness programmes.

The market strategies help to increase the demand of Oxfam through learning outcomes about global issues, concerns and activities related to the problem. The communication approach of marketing is mainly dependent on the relationship towards the target market of the organisation. The organisation utilise the several diverse form of communication like communities, educational sector and local government. The communication medium is used in this process can be advertisement, press, website and seminars (prezi.com, 2015).

2.5 Limitations and Constraints of Marketing

2.5.1 Limitations and Constraints

Sales of Goods Act 1979

According to this act, any goods sold to the customers should be undamaged and will be in good working order. The quality of the good should be satisfactory. The product or service must be sold to the customers as same it was described initially by the marketers. For that marketers have to demonstrate the product correctly and they should make the customers understand the product they are buying.

The act is also applied between the businesses sale. Customers of Tesco can return their goods in exchange of or for their money back through the Tesco 28 day's policy.

Consumer Protection from Unfair Trading Regulation 2008

This regulation has come into force from 26 may 2008. The law implement the Unfair Commercial Practices Directive (UCPD). This regulation has replaced a number of consumer protection legislation.

The main objective of this regulation is that the traders should act honestly and fairly towards their customers. The main aim of Tesco is also to treat their customer well.

Consumerism

Nowadays consumerism has become a social movement for the consumers over the big businesses. Consumerism has given power to the consumers over Tesco. For the consumers, Tesco should produce products of good quality and should keep in consideration that the products should be safe. Tesco should inform their customers if there is any problem related to the product and should also hear complaints of their clients.

Consumer Protection (Distance selling) Regulation 2000

This regulation protects the consumer's rights when they buy products from distant, for example over the phone or the internet. The regulations set information for the seller about the offer on goods or services. Regulation includes:

- Description about the products and services
- Price of the products and services
- Information about the delivery and any cancellation rights
- Detail about the seller.

2.6 Voluntary Code of Advertising in Practice

The act covers mainly six areas, they are as follows:

1. The advertisement should be decent and anything offensive cannot be included in the advertisement.
2. The advertisement should be truthful in context to the price and testimonial should relate and associated with the product.
3. The voluntary code includes health claims, by which the advertisement is restricted by ASA. According to this act, the advertisement cannot include certain diseases and constraints.
4. The act also concerns about the safety measures such as the advertisement should not contain any element which can encourage the viewers to break laws.
5. According to this act, an advertisement is restricted from showing unhealthy and excessive eating.

6. The advertisement should be environment-friendly and should not contain any aspect which can harm the environment (Gray, 2007).

2.7 Marketing Research for Marketing Planning

2.7.1 Impact of Marketing Research in Market Plan

Quantitative and Qualitative Market Research

The quantitative and qualitative market research facilitate the establishment to understand the capability and approach of the market. The quantitative market research mainly deals with the measurement of the different aspects of the market such as market size, brand shares, brand awareness, distribution levels and purchase frequencies. Qualitative market research deals with understanding the element of the market which can influence the performance of an organisation rather than measuring the data for analysis. Tesco has adopted several measures to improve their value for money offers. The organisation has taken initiatives to measure and identify the long-term perspective of different groups of customer. This research work is structured in every two years interval involves asking about the product and services (Self, 2013).

Primary & Secondary Market Research

The market research of Tesco can be classified into primary and secondary research. The Quantitative and Qualitative market research carried by the organisation itself to analyse the market scenario can be termed as primary research. The primary research is much more authentic and specific to the needs of the organisation.

The primary research is directly operated by the company in satisfying various required aspects organised by the establishment. The primary market search is very helpful for an organisation, as the process links the corporation and the buyer directly with higher control quality.

The process is usually cost more to the organisation and takes a longer time to collect information from the market. To lower the cost of research, Tesco outsource the activity to other organisation, which is usually a quick and cheaper process. The secondary market research is not specific and data can be too old. Therefore, analysing the outcome of the primary and secondary market research helps to design effective future marketing strategies.

2.7.2 Limitations of Marketing Research

The limitations of the marketing research are discussed below:

- **Costly:** The process of marketing research in an establishment is an expensive affair. The practice requires a huge workforce and lot of money to conduct various activities. The company have to allocate fund for paying salaries to the working staffs, for preparing questionnaires, conducting surveys and to prepare a report of the research. The process is very complicated and needs skilled professional to analyse the outcome of the research.

- **Time-consuming:** The process of survey and making the final report is a very lengthy procedure. The process involves many complex steps and a single mistake in this process can create an adverse effect to the business operation. The process takes three to six month of time to complete the whole procedure. There is no shortcut or easier way for any urgent scenarios.

- **Limited scope:** The marketing research has a limited scope in solving the business related issues. The research process is unable to solve each and every problem related to customer's behaviour, expenditure, income and relationship, etc.

- **Limited practical Value:** The research is mainly based on the academic aspects, therefore, not capable to fetch a practical solution to the problems. It is a hypothetical approach and gives only theoretical solutions. The solutions are harder to implement on a practical platform (Starcevic, 2013).

- **Unable to predict customer's behaviour:** The research process is not accurate on data and information as the research cannot measure the complex behavioural approach of the consumers. The trend of the market cannot be measured as the behaviours of the customers depends on various aspects such as economic, social, religious, family and many others elements.

- The research on marketing is not a physical science rather a social science. It is highly unpredictable to conclude the buyer's behaviour and marketing environment.

- The marketing research provides mainly suggestion rather than a perfect solution which can be implemented for the successful business. The factors involve in concluding the research is unpredictable, therefore accurate result cannot be obtained.

- In the process of marketing research, the availability of technical staff is a major issue in conducting the research operation. In some scenarios, a non-technical and non-experienced member in marketing research work hampers the outcomes of the research and analysis (Winer, 2000).

- The marketing managers in some cases don't implement the suggestion of research report. Therefore, the process is totally depended on the effective utilisation of the research statement by the marketing managers.

2.8 Marketing Research Influencing Factors in Marketing

There are several factors influence the marketing strategies of the organisation. Some of the crucial factors are listed below

1. The longevity and quality of the product and services are essential for a sustainable development.

2. The analysis and evaluation of the behaviour of the customers approach help in establishing effective strategies in marketing management.

3. The marketing research helps in understanding the position of the organisation in the market which influences the customer to recognise the organisation to meet their desired needs.

4. The marketing research helps in evaluation of the competitive level in the market, therefore organisation can design effective product and services to according to the requirements of the customers.

5. The effective utilisation of organisational resource helps to create a positive and effective planning in an appropriate direction (Palmer, 2004).

2.9 Implementation, Evaluation & Control in Marketing Plan

In the process of marketing management, there are three essential elements for the successful business operation, these are implementation, evaluation and control of the marketing plan. To achieve the respective goal, Tesco has a higher concern about the control and evaluation of their marketing strategies.

The initial step of implementation is very important in marketing management as it make sure that the marketing activities is effectively structured and happens in real time and situation (Zineldin, 2000). The implementation can be done through website launch, running advertisements or through sending emails. Evaluation of the marketing plan is the quantitative and qualitative metrics related with the implementation and strategy.

Quantitative factors include sales leads obtained, amount achieved and customer reached. Therefore, the organisation achieved strategic objective through evaluation can be repeated for future perspective. Effective control over the strategic planning helps to improve the performance and output of the organisation.

2.10 SWOT Analysis

Strength

- Tesco captured a leading position in the UK.
- Solid cash reserves with sales are approximately £72 billion.
- Effective marketing strategies help the organisation to extend their business operation.
- Efficient and technologically advanced business resources.
- Adaptive quality helps to sustain effectively in the competitive platform (McDaniel and Gates, 2012).

Weaknesses

- Over dependence on the local market of UK.
- Unstable financial profit level.
- Free flow of cash is limited.

- Recent controversies created a negative impact on the brand image.

Opportunities

- Rebranding through digital media advertisement and promotion.
- Alignment acquisition with other small chains for sustainable development.
- Development of private label growth.
- Increase of non-food sales.

Threats

- Increase in cost of operation.
- Due to the crisis in the market, the sale is continuously declining.
- Globalisation is increasing the competition in the market.

3.0 Customer Segmentation

The customer segmentation practice is a process dividing the base of the customer into groups which are similar in their perspective toward the organisation. The customer segmentation is done on the basis of interest, age, gender and spending habits. It can be also represented by the business to business and business to customer relationship. The individual customer has various needs therefore it is easier for an organisation to create segmented platform for various types of requirements for different customers. Tesco has divided their customers through segmentation strategy for selling their computer related products:

1. **Family:** Basically for general education, basic games and access to internet. Features require less and budget is average.

2. **Small Office**: For small office or home office requires a little more specifications for various office related work like broad band accesses to the computer, business software, fax and other connectivity to the computer.

3. **Specialist use:** It requires higher performance computer with higher quality of software and hardware. The application in this purpose mainly used for designing, printing, digital image processing and for various complicated works.

4. **Gaming:** The purpose of this segment can be satisfied with Multimedia games, high quality display and sound, peripherals like joystick, broadband Internet access and a powerful processor.

5. **Bulk Supply:** For larger quantity of product for offices, hotels, schools and universities which requires only essential requirements. The organisation focuses on the bulk supply for maximum profit.

6. **Budget segment:** This segment helps to satisfy the needs of the budget customers, which helps the organisation to improve their brand image.

3.0.1 Benefits of Segmentation

- Improve customer service.

- Identify new product.

- Helps to recognise most and least profitable business.

- Effective use of resources.

- Improve the product according to the needs.

- Avoiding the market which is not profitable.

3.1 Marketing Mix for a Product

The marketing mix is the tools used by the marketer to influence users demand. The four elements of marketing mix help to grow the business of an organisation. The four elements are product, promotion, price and place for all the products and services offered by the company. These factors help the organisation to identify the need of the customers related to the purchase and the quality of the product.

There are three more factors which help the company for competing with other companies. The factors are people, physical evidence and purchasing of the product. Therefore, the company mainly aims to provide the best quality of products and services to their customers. Tesco uses each element of the marketing mix for satisfying their customers in order to increase their sales. For example, Tesco introduces the product seven seas extra high strength cod liver oil.

For the success of the product, it is essential to study all the segments of the marketing mix (Dess, 2012).

3.1.1 Product

Seven Seas pure cod liver oil consist of 525 mg of pure cod liver oil, omega 3 nutrients 120mg. The other ingredients of the product include vitamin A and vitamin D3 and also capsule shell. The dosage recommendation of the product is one capsule with the liquid each day. The product market testing is done through various contemporary methods for increasing the efficiency of the product. The product will get a competitive edge over their competitors due to their quality control.

3.1.2 Price

Tesco develops their pricing strategy according to their business strategy. The pricing strategy of Tesco provides a competitive advantage to them over their competitor. Their pricing strategy is based on the marketing message of the company which says "Every Little Helps". The supervision of Tesco decides to offer the cost advantage to their customers by reducing the product price and the operational cost.

They have reduced the operational cost and product price through the economy of the sale and other measures. This policy will help to attract a number of customers and will help in increasing the sale. The price of Seven Seas pure cod liver oil is considered on the basis of the price of the product of competitors.

3.1.3 Place

Marketing mix includes place factor which is related to the customer's location. Seven Seas pure cod liver oil should be targeted in those markets where there is a lack of vitamin A and vitamin D, in general, food habits because of non-availability and high cost. The target customers should be the mothers as they will be interested in supplementing cod liver oil in their children diet (Kotler, 2000).

3.1.4 Promotion

The main marketing objective of Tesco is to increase their profit in the short term as well as in long-term measure and also to increase their brand image. The promotional tools used by the company to achieve the goals include advertisements, event sponsorships, supporting charitable causes and also announcements of new offers and the discounts. Tesco club card is used for collecting information about customer behaviour so that company can use that information for increasing their sales.

3.2 Coherent Marketing Mix for a Product

4Ps are always related in any sorts of coherent marketing mix. In this context, you should consider price, place, product and promotion at the time of developing coherent marketing mix for a product. To understand the marketing process, we can analyze the following example that critically explain the coherent marketing mix process:

The product that my college should provide is the cheap stationery products like books, pens, copies, etc. I have chosen this product specifically because in an educational institution the most used products are books, stationary and copies. So the demand of this product is obviously more than any other products (McDaniel, Lamb and Hair, 2011). This product will get more profit under low capital, which makes this a favorable product to sell in my college. The target of my product is obviously the academic community (e.g. students and teachers).

They are the main element of any educational institution and also are the eager and the perfect buyers for my chosen product (Järvinen and Taiminen, 2015). The aim of the sale of this product is to sell at a low price to a big group or community. Thus, the price of the product will be cheap that even the students who have insolvency can buy it (McDaniel, Lamb and Hair, 2011). The cheap price of product will encourage the students to buy it and will eventually get popular again if the price is low the demand will obviously be greater and so the best decision is to sell the product at such a reasonable price that students of all sorts of financial condition can buy it.

By creating innovative, attractive and colorful posters, brochure, ads in the school magazine, flyers or the particular fan page in social media and also by giving free products in the inauguration day we can promote the products. These steps will help in promontory work and also in advertisement.

The best place to sell my product is in such a place where all the students will be able to acknowledge its existence and will be easily visible.

So the best place would be is in the side of the main entrance of the college. The reason why this is a favorable spot is that not only the students of our college will be able to see it but also students from other college will also be able to see it. And so the sale of the product will be increased a lot. Some of the other reasons are, it is located near the main entrance it will be visible to all the students, which in another case for selecting the location.

Since, it's in the college vicinity the students can get an easy and less time taking access to our products and another maybe the fact that the students do not have to worry about going out of campus to buy these products. And for all these reasons, I think my stationery products are the most suitable one for our institution. My product which is the stationery products, it's designed to appeal to the group of students and the teachers as well. The students and teachers are the basic elements of an educational institution.

As they come to study, they will obviously need things like books, copies, pen, pencil etc. And so our product will already be a popular demand and also appeal to them because my products will be sold at a reasonable price (McDaniel, Lamb and Hair, 2011). And because of this cheap price my product will be in more demand and the sale of it will increase rapidly.

Even students with insolvency will be able to purchase my product and will also get it at a good quality. So my product's appeal will be a good quality product in less price. Now the most important element of the marketing mix for my product that I think is the advertisements and promontory work.

The worst thing for a business is, it's not being known, so if people know about my product it will help to increase the sale and also its demand will rise. Again, there is no use of having a business like this without it being known to any one because the more the people know the better it will be for the business (Järvinen and Taiminen, 2015). And so this is why I think this is such a vital element.

4.0 References

Boothby, K. (2007). Tesco Stores Limited: The IDM Business Performance Awards 2006, Silver Award Winner and Innovation Winner Campaign: Tesco Clubcard — Simpler and more rewarding. *J Direct Data Digit Mark Pract*, 9(2), pp.191-197.

Campaignlive.co.uk, (2015). *Oxfam launches review of UK direct marketing.* [Online] Available at: http://www.campaignlive.co.uk/article/1308669/oxfam-launches-review-uk-direct-marketing [Accessed 29 Nov. 2015].

Czinkota, M. and Kotabe, M. (2001). *Marketing management.* Cincinnati: South-Western College Pub.

Cargill.com, (2015). *Cargill: Our company..* [online] Available at: http://www.cargill.com/company/ [Accessed 14 Dec. 2015].

Dann, S. and Dann, S. (2004). *Introduction to marketing.* Milton, Qld.: Wiley.

Dess, G. (2012). *Strategic management.* New York: McGraw-Hill/Irwin.

Gray, S. (2007). Voluntary marketing codes: The UK ABPI Code of Practice and its implications for the proposed Code of Practice for the Promotion of NHS Services. *Journal of Management & Marketing in Healthcare*, 1(1), pp.54-60.

Kotler, P. (2000). *Marketing management.* Upper Saddle River, N.J.: Prentice Hall.

Järvinen, J. and Taiminen, H. (2015). Harnessing marketing automation for B2B content marketing. *Industrial Marketing Management*.

Lewis, T. (1999). *Microsoft rising--and other tales of Silicon Valley*. Los Alamitos, Calif.: IEEE Computer Society.

McDaniel, C. and Gates, R. (2012). *Marketing research essentials*. Hoboken, N.J.: Wiley.

Microsoft.com, (2015). *Microsoft – Official Home Page*. [online] Available at: http://www.microsoft.com/ [Accessed 14 Dec. 2015].

Palmer, M. (2004). International Retail Restructuring and Divestment: The Experience of Tesco. *Journal of Marketing Management*, 20(9-10), pp.1075-1105.

prezi.com, (2015). *The Oxfam marketing strategy*. [Online] Available at: https://prezi.com/b7mf8nmlviwt/the-oxfam-marketing-strategy/ [Accessed 29 Nov. 2015].

Rossiter, J. (2002). Introduction to the Special Issue on marketing Knowledge.*Marketing Theory*, 2(4), pp.331-332.

Self, D. (2013). *Public Mental Health Marketing*. Hoboken: Taylor and Francis.

Starcevic, S. (2013). Research of brand personality concept in marketing.*Marketing*, 44(2), pp.149-172.

Winer, R. (2000). *Marketing management*. Upper Saddle River, N.J.: Prentice Hall.

Wood, M. (2012). Marketing social marketing. *Journal of Social Marketing*, 2(2), pp.94-102.

Zineldin, M. (2000). Beyond relationship marketing: technologicalship marketing. *Marketing Intelligence & Planning*, 18(1), pp.9-23.

About the Author

Ghazi Mokammel Hossain is a freelance writer. He has written some books as well as articles, research papers and creative articles. The author is also working in different type of researcher projects. He was born on 31 December, 1993. He has passed his S.S.C exam in 2008 and passed H.S.C exam in 2010. He has graduated with a Bachelor's of Business Administration (BBA) in HRM in 2015 from a renowned University. He has also completed Social Compliance & CSR diploma in 2016.

He published his first book called "IPv4 IP6 Technology & Implementation" in Amazon Kindle and Createspace on 201. After that, he has already been published different books on various subjects.
The author published an outstanding thrilling novel called "Anwar: Emergence of Unknown Defenders" in 2016 on Amazon kindle and Createspace. Playing football, Cricket, PC games, reading books, novel, research paper, cycling and mountain climbing are his favorite hobbies.

Also By Ghazi Mokammel Hossain & GM Publishers

Supermarket Management Practices: In the Changing Economic Environment- November, 2016 by Ghazi Mokammel Hossain
https://www.amazon.com/dp/B01MFGHM6X

Anwar: Emergence of Unknown Defenders- August 10, 2016 by Ghazi Mokammel Hossain
https://www.amazon.com/dp/B01K8KLIJ8

The Survival of USA – Part Two: A Novel - August, 2016 by Ghazi Mokammel Hossain & MD. Fazle Mubin
https://www.amazon.com/dp/B01K8I4Z0E

Business Environment: Theoretical & Organizational Aspects – July, 2016 by Ghazi Mokammel Hossain
https://www.amazon.com/dp/B01HTQYG7A

The Survival of USA - Part One: A Novel – March, 2016 by Ghazi Mokammel Hossain, MD. Fazle Mubin & Pranjal Rahman
https://www.amazon.com/dp/B01CTXNF8E

Enterprise IPv6 for Enterprise Networks- December, 2015 by Ghazi Mokammel Hossain & Fathe Mubin
https://www.amazon.com/dp/B017U84ISO

Heart of Democracy: A Versatile Poetry Book - Aug 28, 2015 by Ghazi Mozammel Hossain
https://www.amazon.com/dp/B014MTHGRY

The Brave Parrot of Jungle - Dec 11, 2014 by Syeda Taskin Ara & Gulshan Ahmed
https://www.amazon.com/dp/B00QXHW4PS

IPv4 IPv6 Technology and Implementation - Nov 2, 2013 by Ghazi Mokammel Hossain & GM Hossain

https://www.amazon.com/dp/B00GEHNC8K

The Mirror of Religion - Jul 19, 2015 by Ghazi Mozammel Hossain & Richard Marks

https://www.amazon.com/dp/B01204RO1O

Introduction to Network on Chip Routing Algorithms - Oct 4, 2014 by Ghazi Mokammel Hossain

https://www.amazon.com/dp/B00O6ET3J0

Ebola Epidemic: A Detail Survival Guide From Ebola Virus Disease Outbreak - Oct 25, 2014 by Ghazi Mokammel Hossain & Dr. Robert Alex

https://www.amazon.com/dp/B00OWG4TL4

Fundamental of API Based Financial Engineering - Oct 17, 2014 by Ghazi Mokammel Hossain

https://www.amazon.com/dp/B00OJJJJO6

For more details please visit Amazon Author Central
https://www.amazon.com/Ghazi-Mokammel-Hossain/ 1

www.ingramcontent.com/pod-product-compliance
Lightning Source LLC
Chambersburg PA
CBHW050026230526
45470CB00003B/1147